LOÏC HANNO

The Griddle Cookbook

DELICIOUS, FLAVOR-PACKED RECIPES FOR FLAT-TOP GRILLING

Photographs: **AIMERY CHEMIN**

Food Stylist: **CHAE RIN VINCENT**

ULYSSES PRESS

First printed in 2020 in France as *Les meilleures recettes de plancha d'ici et d'ailleurs* by Mango

Published in the US by:
Ulysses Press
PO Box 3440
Berkeley, CA 94703
www.ulyssespress.com

ISBN: 978-1-64604-144-2
Library of Congress Control Number: 2020946981

Printed in the United States by Versa Press
10 9 8 7 6 5 4 3 2 1

Text: Loïc Hanno
Photos: Aimery Chemin
Styling: Chae Rin Vincent
Cover photo: Aimery Chemin
US editors: Renee Rutledge and Barbara Schultz

CONTENTS

INTRODUCTION

Cooking on the griddle is easier than it seems. During my travels, I discovered the extraordinary variety of flavors that a griddle can bring out in food from all over the world. It's my goal to share what I've learned from these journeys so you, too, can explore a simple, healthy, and rich way of cooking.

LOÏC HANNO

Loïc Hanno grew up in the 10th arrondissement of Paris. On Wednesday afternoons, he visited the Strasbourg-Saint-Denis district to taste authentic shawarmas and falafels. He also visited Belleville, where he feasted on pho soup and any other Asian specialties he uncovered. Suffice it to say, he tasted global flavors without crossing a single border! As an adult, he traveled extensively and frequented restaurant kitchens around the world, and then returned home full of memories with a thousand flavors.

THE BASICS

In addition to selecting choice ingredients, it's very important to apply precise cooking methods when using the griddle to avoid tough meat, dry fish, or soggy vegetables.

Using an electric or cast-iron griddle is simple, with just a few essential techniques and a convenient cooking method. Make sure your knives are sharp so you can precisely chop, cut, and slice your ingredients and minimize the risk of injury. Remember: always degrease the griddle after use, and—above all—share your griddle cooking with friends!

Utensils

Citrus juicer

Ginger grater

Oil cruet

Mortar and pestle

Cutting board

Angled spatula

Stainless steel tongs

Brush

Paring knife

Stainless steel clamp

Melting dome

Double spatula

Electric griddle

Spatula

9

Tamarind paste

Garlic

Worcestershire sauce

Ginger

Banana leaves

Lemongrass

Jalapeño peppers

Tandoori spices

Cilantro

Tahini

Bird's eye chile

Red curry paste

Rice vinegar

Kalamata olives

Sate

Garam masala

Pomegranate molasses

Shrimp paste

Peanuts

Moroccan chile

Dried bonito flakes

Limes

Oyster sauce

Coconut milk

Green peppercorns

Bok choy

Asian beer

Gochujang

Sake

Turmeric

Makrut lime leaves

Smoked paprika

Napa cabbage

Sesame oil

Sumac

Fish sauce

A Quick Overview

COOKING TIME
(in minutes)

		Rare	Medium rare	Well done
Meat	Lamb (chops)		6	8
	Lamb (kefta)	5	6	
	Beef (steak)	6	6.5	8
	Beef (rump steak)		7	8
	Duck (breast)		25	
	Pork (loin)		15	
	Pork (grilled)		12	
	Pork (grilled—pieces)		6	
	Chicken thighs (boneless)		11	
	Chicken breast (fillet)		8	
	Chicken breast (pieces)		4	
Seafood	Sea bass / lean 1½ pounds		34	
	Sea bass / lean (tenderloin)		15	
	Shrimp		2	
	Cockles		5	
	Sea bream / 1½ pounds		34	
	Sea bream (fillet)		15	
	Langoustines		1	
	Clams		5	

TOOLS

All you need for the griddle are one or two spatulas and a melting dome (also known as a steaming or basting cover). Using spatulas with shellfish requires a certain amount of dexterity. The melting dome traps steam around the food to speed up cooking (for example, preparing eggplant without the dome would require at least 15 minutes and much more oil to avoid burning).

USING THE GRIDDLE

Most griddles concentrate heat in the center (where the burner is located) rather than along the edges. You can use the sides of the griddle for very light cooking or to keep food warm. Gentle or low heat on a griddle is 230–300°F, medium heat is near 400°F, and high heat is up to 520°F.

FOOD PREP AND REST

Remove any refrigerated ingredients 20 minutes before you begin a recipe to ensure even cooking. Otherwise, the center of your meat might not cook properly.

When meat is cooking, its blood concentrates in the center. After cooking, it moves back to the edges and flows onto the plate. This is why you must let the cooked meat rest, covered at room temperature, for at least half of its cooking time. This way, it will be tender (because the blood will have permeated throughout the meat) and you will avoid having a reddish pool of juices at the bottom of the plate.

Cooking fish also requires careful attention. An overcooked fish forms albumin on its surface (a white liquid with the texture and color of wood glue), which indicates that the fish is drying out. So pay attention to the formation of white pearls on your fish while cooking; if these appear, it's a good indication of overcooking. Finally, fish is always better when the flesh looks slightly iridescent.

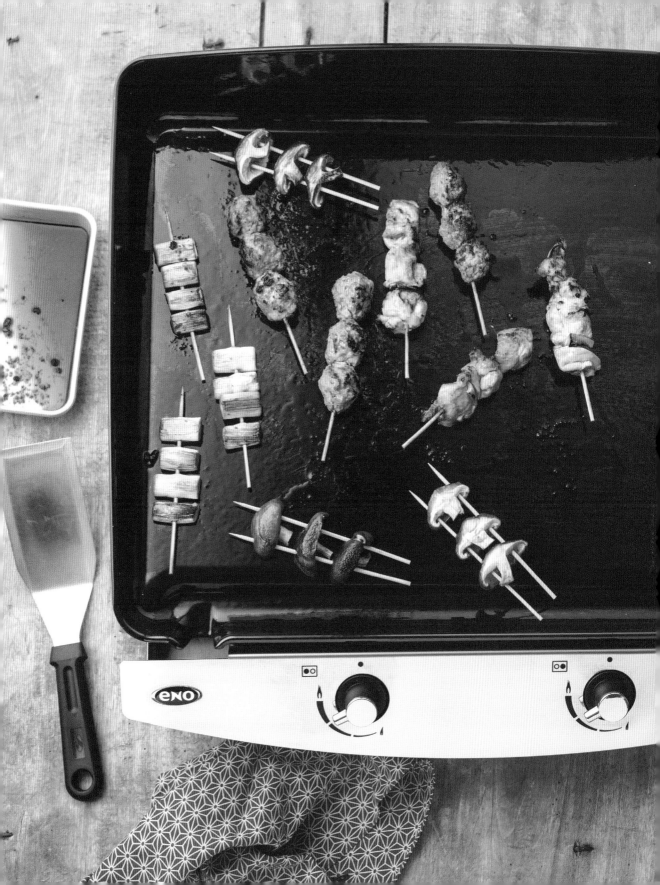

PREPARING SHRIMP FOR THE GRIDDLE

To prepare shrimp easily:

1. If the shrimp are headless, poke a toothpick or insert the tip of a knife at the end of the tail. Gently pull to separate the flesh from the shell without breaking it. Detach the rest of the shell with a firm pull.

2. If the shrimp are head-on, remove the last ring from the tail then insert a toothpick at the end of the tail. Gently pull to separate the flesh from the shell without breaking it. Detach the rest of the shell with a firm pull.

To prevent shrimp from shrinking:

Shell the shrimp. Place a shrimp on its stomach. Using your thumb, press down on the shrimp to break the muscles at each end and in the middle. Repeat with the remaining shrimp.

Cook the shrimp on high heat for 1 minute maximum on each side. They are cooked when their flesh is pink and barely opaque in the center. Shrimp usually have more flavor when they are cooked in their shells. However, with this method, the shrimp can be difficult to eat later, especially for children.

PREPARING LANGOUSTINES FOR THE GRIDDLE

To remove the heads, start by gently pulling the head of a langoustine until it slips free from the casing.

Lightly press up and down the sides of the langoustine to loosen the shell from the body.

Spread the shell apart so it lies on either side of the body.

Remove the shell to make detaching the head easier. Repeat with the remaining langoustines.

The langoustines cook for a maximum of 45 seconds on each side at high heat. They are finished cooking when their flesh is pink and slightly pearly in the center. Langoustines are more flavorful when cooked with their shells on, but they can be annoying to peel and eat at the table, and you'll risk catapulting a claw or the like into your mother-in-law's eye!

PREPARING SCALLOPS FOR THE GRIDDLE

Use a paring knife to cut under the adductor muscle (the edible white part). Then, using the flat part of the blade, separate the adductor muscle from the shell.

Pass the knife blade under the organs to detach and push them out of the shell.

Cut and remove the membrane around the adductor muscle, as well as the rectum. Cut the edible orange coral, also referred to as "the roe."

Rinse the scallops under a stream of cool water, and dry.

Scallops are best cooked for 2 minutes on each side at medium heat. To test for doneness, press down on the top of one with your finger. The flesh should feel firmer, but flexible.

PREPARING CHICKEN FOR THE GRIDDLE

For an experienced chef, a chicken thigh can be deboned in less than a minute. If this is your first time, however, it will likely take about 3 minutes per thigh.

The thigh is the easiest and most flavorful piece of chicken to cook. Because it has more fat than white meat, it has a softer texture that helps reduce the risk of overcooking and becoming dry (we have all eaten a chicken breast that was close to suffocating us because it was so dry).

Using a small, sharp knife, cut the skin at the end of the thigh, making a hole between the skin and flesh.

Follow the thigh bone (fibula) with the knife to loosen the flesh from the bone.

Follow the drumstick bone (femur) with the knife to loosen the flesh from the bone.

Chicken often contains Staphylococci, which can make you sick for a whole weekend if ingested, so always cook your chicken thoroughly. If the center is pink, continue cooking.

In addition to adding flavor to your meat, using a marinade can tenderize the chicken, especially if it contains oil. If your piece of meat is lean (like a chicken breast), don't hesitate to let it marinate in order to limit the risk of it drying out.

PREPARING VEGETABLES FOR THE GRIDDLE

Vegetables are perfect for giving your dish more volume and color, but they are very easy to overcook. Nothing is sadder than a bunch of soggy vegetables on a plate—so make sure they stay crunchy (except for eggplant). If you want to brighten the vegetables' colors, you can bleach them for 1 minute in boiling water with 1 tablespoon of baking soda, or boil in sparkling water.

ZUCCHINI

For easy cooking, cut the zucchini lengthwise in 4 or 5 slices. If you want to sauté the zucchini, it's best to cut them into 2-inch-long sections, then quarter them.

EGGPLANT (CUT 1)

Eggplant soaks up oil very easily. To avoid serving oil-soaked eggplant, first cut it into ½-inch thick slices, brush the olive oil on the slices, and then cook for 5 minutes on each side at medium heat under a melting dome. For faster cooking, you can also steam the eggplant.

EGGPLANT (CUT 2)

Cut the eggplant into ½-inch long slices. This cut works well for grilled vegetable salad.

RED CABBAGE

This vegetable is tough and hard to chew. Using a sharp knife, slice it into very thin pieces.

PEPPER

Cut the pepper in half, then remove the seeds and the white parts. Slice into thin quarters.

AROMATIC HERBS

Using a sharp knife, chop up a handful of herbs, being careful not to crush them too much in order to maintain the maximum freshness and essential oils.

FENNEL

Cut thin slices lengthwise from the bulb. Keep the leaves, which can be used to flavor a vinaigrette or decorate the plates.

Sauces

Dog sauce

Mango sauce

Sate sauce

Peanut sauce

24

Mojo sauce

Gremolata
sauce

Barbecue
sauce

Sauces

DOG SAUCE

About 1 cup of sauce

- ¼ bunch flat-leaf parsley, chopped
- 4 green onions, sliced
- 1 chile pepper, chopped
- juice of 1 lime
- ½ cup hot water
- 1 teaspoon sugar
- 2 pinches salt

In a bowl, combine all the ingredients, except the parsley.

Once the sauce has cooled, add the parsley and mix.

MANGO SAUCE

About 1 cup of sauce

- 3 sprigs cilantro, leaves separated and stems removed
- 2 sprigs mint, leaves separated and stems removed
- 1 large mango, peeled and chopped
- 1 shallot, chopped
- ½ Thai chile pepper, chopped
- ½ cup cider vinegar or rice vinegar

Place all the ingredients into a food processor and blend until the mixture becomes smooth.

SATE SAUCE

About 1 cup of sauce

- 1 chile pepper
- 2 shallots, chopped
- 2 cloves garlic, minced
- olive oil or vegetable oil for cooking
- 2 tablespoons peanuts
- 0.4 inch fresh ginger, chopped
- ½ teaspoon five-spice
- 2½ teaspoons sugar
- 3 pinches salt
- 3 grinds black pepper

Preheat the griddle to medium heat. Cook the pepper for 3 minutes. Set aside for later.

Fry the shallots on the griddle until crispy. Drain them on a paper towel.

Finally, cook the garlic on the griddle at low heat with a drizzle of oil for about 90 seconds.

In a container, crush the peanuts and mix with the rest of the ingredients.

PEANUT SAUCE

About 1 cup of sauce

- ¼ cup peanuts
- 1 shallot, chopped
- ¼ cup sunflower or peanut oil
- 2 cloves garlic, chopped
- 1⅓ cups coconut milk

On the griddle, roast the peanuts for 3 minutes at medium heat. Set aside on a plate.

Fry the chopped shallot on the griddle in hot oil until crispy. Drain the oil, then cook the garlic for 1 minute at low heat.

Mix the peanuts, shallot, and garlic with the coconut milk until it reaches the consistency of a smooth sauce.

MOJO SAUCE

About 1 cup of sauce

- 2 cloves garlic, chopped
- 3 tablespoons olive oil
- ½ bunch flat-leaf parsley
- 2 tablespoons ground coriander
- juice of 2 oranges
- juice of 1 lime
- 1 teaspoon hot paprika

Place the chopped garlic in a bowl. Gently heat the olive oil in a saucepan, then pour it over the garlic. Let cool.

Add the herbs, citrus juice, and pepper to the garlic oil and mix everything together.

BARBECUE SAUCE

About 1 cup of sauce

- 1 onion, chopped
- 1 poblano, cayenne, or other mild to moderately hot pepper, chopped
- 10 tablespoons ketchup
- 1 tablespoon mustard
- 2 tablespoons Worcestershire sauce
- 2 tablespoons honey
- ½ cup water
- 6 tablespoons apple cider vinegar
- ¼ cup brown sugar
- 1 teaspoon black peppercorns, crushed

Place all the ingredients in a saucepan. Heat until boiling, then cook for 45 minutes over low heat, stirring regularly.

Mix the sauce thoroughly and let cool.

GREMOLATA SAUCE

About 1 cup of sauce

- ¼ bunch flat-leaf parsley, chopped
- 1 clove garlic, minced
- zest and juice of 1 lemon
- juice of ½ orange

In a bowl, combine the parsley and garlic. Add the lemon zest and juice, then the orange juice. Mix well.

Sauce vierge

Aji sauce

Tarator sauce

Chimichurri

Sauces

Onion sauce

Adobo sauce

Spring onion
sauce

Sauces

SAUCE VIERGE

About 1 cup of sauce

- 3 tomatoes
- 1 stalk celery with lower end discarded, cut into ¼-inch cubes
- ½ bunch basil, chopped
- 5 kalamata olives, cut into small cubes
- juice of ¼ lemon
- ¼ cup olive oil
- 2 tablespoons white balsamic vinegar

Boil the tomatoes for 30 seconds, then drain, peel, and cut them into ¼-inch cubes.

In a bowl, combine all the ingredients.

AJI SAUCE

About 1 cup of sauce

- 1 onion, sliced
- 2 cloves garlic, chopped
- ½ cup baked potato
- 1 Moroccan chile, sliced
- 1 orange, supremed (pith removed and sliced)
- 1 tablespoon olive oil

On the griddle, fry the onion in half of the olive oil for 1 minute, then drain it and set aside. Cook the garlic on the griddle with the remaining oil for 30 seconds at medium heat.

Place the onion and garlic in a food processor. Add the rest of the ingredients and blend to a smooth consistency.

TARATOR SAUCE

About 1 cup of sauce

- 3 tablespoons tahini
- juice of 1 lemon
- 1 clove garlic, minced
- ½ cup water
- 2 pinches salt

In a bowl, mix the tahini with the rest of the ingredients to make a smooth sauce.

CHIMICHURRI

About 1 cup of sauce

- 2 shallots, sliced
- ½ bunch flat-leaf parsley, chopped
- ½ bunch basil, chopped
- 2 tablespoons fresh chopped cilantro
- 1 clove garlic, mashed
- 1 tablespoon oregano
- 2 pinches hot paprika
- 6 tablespoons olive oil
- 3 tablespoons cider vinegar or rice vinegar

In a bowl, combine the shallots, herbs, and garlic. Add the remaining ingredients and mix thoroughly.

ONION SAUCE

About 1 cup of sauce

- 1 teaspoon sesame seeds
- 2 cloves garlic, chopped
- 1 dried chile or 1 teaspoon chile powder
- 1 bay leaf
- 1 teaspoon sugar
- 1 tablespoon peanuts (a small handful)
- 1 teaspoon cornstarch
- 1 teaspoon dried oregano
- 2 pinches salt
- ¼ cup cider vinegar or rice vinegar
- ½ cup chicken broth
- 3 onions, chopped
- 3 tablespoons olive oil

In a bowl, smash the sesame seeds with the garlic, chile pepper, bay leaf, sugar, and peanuts. Add the cornstarch, oregano, and salt. Mix in the vinegar and chicken broth.

Preheat the griddle to medium heat. Then brown the onions in the olive oil for about 3 minutes. Add the broth mixture, using a spatula to prevent it from spilling out. Let cook for 3 minutes, then serve warm.

ADOBO SAUCE

About 1 cup of sauce

- ¾ cup ancho, chipotle, or guajillo peppers
- 1 clove garlic
- 4 sprigs cilantro
- ½ teaspoon ground cumin
- ⅔ cup cider vinegar or rice vinegar
- 1 tablespoon sugar
- 3 pinches salt

Rehydrate the peppers in boiling water for 20 to 30 minutes. Core the peppers and cut them in half lengthwise. Flatten them with the blade of a knife. Place them on the griddle skin side down and grill them at low heat for about 8 minutes.

Scrape off the pulp of the peppers into a food processor and add in the other ingredients. Blend until the sauce reaches a smooth consistency.

SPRING ONION SAUCE

About 1 cup of sauce

- 1 jalapeño or Moroccan chile, minced
- 1 bunch spring onions, minced
- juice of 5 limes
- ¼ cup sugar

In a bowl, mix the jalapeño (or Moroccan chile) and onion with the lime juice, then add the sugar.

Marinades

Ponzu

Barbecue

Tikka

Shawarma

Churrasqueira

Churrasco

Marinades

PONZU

About 1 cup of marinade

- 2 cloves garlic, chopped
- ¾-inch fresh ginger, chopped
- juice of ½ lime
- 8 tablespoons soy sauce
- 6 tablespoons mirin

In a bowl, combine the chopped garlic and ginger with the remaining ingredients.

TIKKA

About 1 cup of marinade

- 3 cloves garlic
- 1½ inches fresh ginger
- 1 chile pepper
- juice of 1 lime
- 1½ cups Greek or Turkish yogurt
- 1½ tablespoons paprika
- 1½ teaspoons turmeric
- 1½ teaspoons garam masala

Mix the garlic and ginger with the chile and lime juice.

Place this mixture in a bowl to marinate for 3 hours. Then add the yogurt and spices. Mix well.

BARBECUE

About 1 cup of marinade

- 1 teaspoon black peppercorns, crushed
- 1 clove garlic, chopped
- ¼ cup ketchup
- ¼ cup Worcestershire sauce
- 1 tablespoon honey
- 1 tablespoon dried oregano
- ¼ cup olive oil
- 2 tablespoons cider vinegar

In a bowl, combine the peppercorns and garlic with the remaining ingredients.

On average, a marinade penetrates meat at a rate of 1 to 2 millimeters per day. A 1-day marination is best when preparing dishes with mild flavors, or dishes that require infusing some acidity into the meat (e.g., shawarma). Otherwise, marinades generally add a lot of flavor without the risk of covering up the taste of the meat or fish, even when you extend the marinating time. For most preparations, marinating the meat for 1 to 2 hours is sufficient.

SHAWARMA

About 1 cup of marinade

- 1½ cups red wine vinegar
- zest and juice of 2 oranges
- zest and juice of 1 lemon
- 2 red onions, sliced
- 4 cloves garlic, crushed
- 1 cinnamon stick, crushed
- 2 bay leaves, crushed
- 2 cloves, crushed
- 1½ teaspoons nutmeg
- 1½ teaspoons coriander seeds, crushed
- 5 grinds black pepper

Pour the vinegar and citrus juice into a bowl. Add the rest of the ingredients and mix.

CHURRASQUEIRA

About 1 cup of marinade

- 2 onions, roughly chopped
- 3 cloves garlic, roughly chopped
- ¼ bunch flat-leaf parsley
- 1 bay leaf
- 1 tablespoon chile pepper or paprika
- 1 cup white wine
- ¼ cup olive oil

Place the onion and garlic in a food processor. Add the rest of the ingredients and mix.

CHURRASCO

About 1 cup of marinade

- ½ bunch flat-leaf parsley, chopped
- 3 cloves garlic, chopped
- 6 tablespoons cider vinegar or rice vinegar
- 6 tablespoons olive oil
- 2 teaspoons sugar
- 2 teaspoons black pepper

In a bowl, combine the parsley with the rest of the ingredients.

Marinades

Tortillas

Churrascaria

Teriyaki

Tandoori

Chermoula

Brazilian

Marinades

TORTILLAS

About 1 cup of marinade

- 1 onion, sliced
- 2 cloves garlic, minced
- 1 chile pepper, sliced
- 1 bay leaf
- 1 teaspoon ground cumin
- 1 teaspoon dried oregano
- juice of 2 limes
- 2 tablespoons olive oil

In a bowl, combine the onion, garlic, and chile pepper. Add the rest of the ingredients and mix.

TERIYAKI

About 1 cup of marinade

- 1 clove garlic, chopped
- about 1 inch fresh ginger, chopped
- ⅔ cup soy sauce
- 3 tablespoons cider vinegar or rice vinegar
- 6 tablespoons sugar

In a bowl, combine the chopped garlic and ginger with the remaining ingredients.

CHURRASCARIA

About 1 cup of marinade

- 1 chile pepper
- 2 cloves garlic
- ⅔ cup pineapple juice
- juice of 2 limes
- 2 tablespoons paprika
- 2 tablespoons olive oil
- 2 grinds black pepper

Mince the chile pepper and garlic and then combine into a paste by pressing and dragging the flat side of a knife across both.

In a bowl, combine the garlic and chile puree with the rest of the ingredients.

TANDOORI

About 1 cup of marinade

- 2 cardamom pods
- 2 pinches ground cinnamon
- ½ teaspoon ground cumin
- 1 teaspoon ground coriander
- 1 clove
- 1 tablespoon paprika
- 1 teaspoon chili powder
- 1 teaspoon garlic powder
- 1 teaspoon black peppercorns
- 6 curry leaves (optional)
- 1½ cups of Greek or Turkish yogurt

Grind up the cardamom seeds with the other spices.

In a container, mix the yogurt with the crushed spices.

BRAZILIAN

About 1 cup of marinade

- 1 tablespoon orange zest
- 2 tablespoons chopped fresh cilantro
- 4 cloves garlic, chopped
- 1 Moroccan pepper, chopped
- juice of 2 oranges
- ¼ cup olive oil

Place the orange zest, cilantro, garlic, and pepper in a bowl.

Add the orange juice and olive oil to the bowl and mix until all of the ingredients are combined.

Garlic is very fragrant, and it can leave a smell on the fingers. To remove that garlic smell, use steel soap or fresh lemon juice when washing your hands.

CHERMOULA

About 1 cup of marinade

- 1 fennel bulb, sliced
- 1 tablespoon cumin seeds
- 1 teaspoon coriander seeds
- 1 onion, chopped
- 1 Moroccan pepper, sliced
- ½ bunch flat-leaf parsley
- 2 tablespoons fresh cilantro
- 1 teaspoon organic ground turmeric
- juice of 2 lemons
- ⅔ cup olive oil
- 1 teaspoon salt
- 1 teaspoon black pepper

Cook the fennel on the griddle at medium heat for 10 minutes until tender.

Roast the cumin and coriander seeds for 1 minute on the griddle at medium heat.

Place all the ingredients in a food processor and blend.

Europe

Griddle cooking, a regional specialty originally from southwest France that has spread throughout the country, combines the best elements of a healthy, simple, and casual cuisine: cooking with little fat, using a limited number of ingredients, and preparing foods simply allow you more leisure time to have a glass of wine with friends while you cook!

These recipes will remind you of the south of France, Lisbon bistros, Andalusian bars, and even Greek tavernas.

DUCK BREASTS WITH OLIVES

Prep time: 10 minutes

Cook time: 26 minutes

Serves 4

- 4 skin-on duck breasts
- ⅔ cup white wine
- 1 cup sun-dried tomatoes, chopped
- ½ cup pitted green olives, chopped
- salt and freshly ground pepper, to taste
- ½ bunch basil
- zest and juice of 1 lemon (optional)

Preheat the griddle to low heat.

Using a knife, make a diamond grid on the duck skin to help render off the fat while the meat cooks.

Place the breasts skin-side down on the griddle for 20 minutes to render the skin.

Increase the heat. Flip and sear for 3 minutes on high heat, then 2 minutes on medium heat.

Lower the heat. Deglaze with white wine and add the tomatoes and olives. Continue cooking for 1 minute.

Add the salt and pepper. After the duck rests, cut it into thin slices, garnish with the fresh basil, and serve hot.

After cooking, add the zest of 1 lemon with its juice to give your dish extra flavor.

MEAGRE
WITH VIRGIN SAUCE

Prep time: 10 minutes

Cook time: 15 minutes

Serves 4

- 2 tablespoons olive oil
- 2 (¾-pound) meagre fillets
- salt and freshly ground pepper, to taste
- 1 cup virgin sauce (page 30)

Preheat the griddle to medium heat, add the oil, and place the fillets skin-side down. Cook for 15 minutes. Sprinkle with salt and pepper.

Serve the fillets hot with the virgin sauce, or sauce vierge.

Get your fillet from your fishmonger, if you can. Instead of meagre, you can also use sea bass, but it is often expensive when caught fresh. This recipe also works with red mullet fillets—cook them for 3 minutes at medium heat.

LANGOUSTINES WITH GREMOLATA

Prep time: 30 minutes

Cook time: About 1 minute

Serves 4

- 3 pounds langoustines
- 3 tablespoons olive oil
- 1 cup gremolata sauce (page 27)
- salt and freshly ground pepper, to taste

While it can take a little more time to prep this dish, it is definitely worth it (and your dinner guests will think so, too).

When you shell the langoustines, do not throw away the shells or heads. Instead, place them in a pot with some olive oil. Then add an onion, 2 cloves of garlic, a stalk of celery, 2 tomatoes, and a thinly sliced leek. Pour in about ½ gallon of water and cook for 1 hour. This will give you an aromatic broth that you can use to prepare other tasty dishes, like a risotto, for example.

Shell the langoustines. Use a toothpick to help remove the casing (see page 18).

On the griddle, cook the langoustines in the olive oil at high heat for about 30 to 45 seconds per side.

Arrange the langoustines on the serving platter, then sprinkle with gremolata. Add salt and pepper to taste.

If you want to cook the langoustines in their shells, allow for 2 more minutes of cooking on each side.

CHORIZO MUSSELS

Prep time: 25 minutes

Cook time: 15 minutes

Serves 4

- 4 pounds mussels
- 4 shallots, minced
- 2 tablespoons olive oil
- 2 cloves garlic, minced
- 8 tomatoes
- 6 celery stalks, tapered then cut into ¾-inch slices
- ¾ cup chorizo, sliced thin then cut into matchsticks
- 1½ cups vinho verde (Portuguese white wine) or white wine of your choice
- ¼ bunch flat-leaf parsley

Wash, sort, and trim the mussels (discard the open ones).

On the griddle, brown the shallots in the olive oil for 2 minutes at medium heat. Add the garlic and sauté for 30 seconds.

Next, add the mussels, tomatoes, celery, and chorizo. Deglaze with the white wine. Mix everything together with a spatula and cook for 10 minutes at low heat, stirring regularly.

Once the mussels are open, sprinkle with parsley and serve immediately.

To add some fruity notes to your dish, you can add hot paprika and ½ cup of fresh grapes, sliced in half.

PORTUGUESE SHRIMP

Prep time: 5 minutes

Cook time: 4 minutes

Serves 4

- 6 cloves garlic, minced
- ⅔ cups olive oil, divided
- 2¼ pounds raw shrimp
- salt and freshly ground pepper, to taste

This dish can be found in any Portuguese bistro. However, beware of the effects of the atmosphere combined with the vinho verde on the side (I was laughing to myself at the end of the meal)!

Place the garlic in a bowl and set aside. Preheat the griddle to medium heat.

Add 2 tablespoons of the olive oil and sear the shrimp for 2 minutes on each side.

While the shrimp cooks, heat the remaining olive oil in a pan on the griddle. Pour the hot oil over the garlic. Add salt and pepper, to taste.

Enjoy the shrimp by dipping them in the seasoned oil.

If you prefer to cook the shrimp without the shell, reduce the cooking time to 1 minute per side.

You can replace the shrimp with prawns.

CHICKEN CHURRASQUEIRA

Prep time: 10 minutes

Marinate time: 6 hours

Cook time: 11 minutes

Serves 4

- 6 chicken thighs, deboned
- 1 cup of churrasqueira marinade (page 35)
- ¼ cup olive oil

This dish is a Portuguese staple, spicy or not. It is traditionally served after a hard day of olive picking—a real delight!

Place the chicken in a deep dish. Cover with the marinade and refrigerate for 6 hours.

Grease the griddle with the oil and preheat it to medium heat.

Drain the chicken and cook, skin-side down, for 7 minutes. Turn the flesh side down and finish cooking for 4 minutes.

For a complete dish, serve with potatoes browned in garlic: cook 1¼ pounds of potatoes for 10 minutes in boiling water. Drain them, then cut the potatoes into slices. Brown them on the griddle with olive oil for 5 minutes on each side. After cooking, add 2 tablespoons of olive oil, the juice of ½ lemon, and 1 clove of chopped garlic. Finish with salt and pepper, to taste.

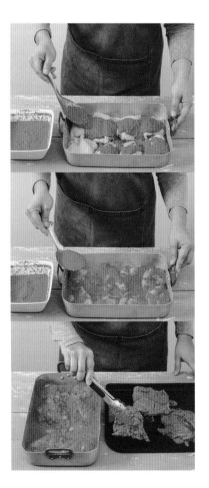

GRILLED PORK
WITH CHILE PEPPER

Prep time: 10 minutes

Marinate time: 2 hours

Cook time: 16 minutes

Serves 4

- 1½ pounds grilled pork
- 1 teaspoon of chile pepper
- 1 teaspoon garlic powder
- 1 bay leaf
- 1 teaspoon oregano
- 1 teaspoon black peppercorns
- ¼ cup olive oil, divided
- ½ small green cabbage, cut into strips
- 1½ tablespoons butter
- 1 glass white wine
- salt and freshly ground pepper, to taste

Cut the grilled pork into 4 pieces. Place them in a deep dish.

In a bowl, mash together the pepper, garlic, and bay leaf. Add the oregano and peppercorns, then toss with half of the olive oil. Pour this marinade over the meat and refrigerate for 2 hours.

Blanch the cabbage in a saucepan of boiling salted water for 1 minute. Drain.

On the griddle, use the remaining olive oil to cook the marinated pork at medium heat for 8 minutes per side (while scraping any attached marinade with a spatula to prevent it from burning).

Halfway through cooking, sauté the cabbage in the butter at medium heat for 3 minutes, then turn up the heat and cook for 5 minutes more. Deglaze with the white wine.

Serve the pork on a bed of cabbage. Add salt and pepper, to taste.

Be careful with the amount of chile pepper; its smoky taste can quickly overpower other flavors! If you accidentally add too much, rebalance your dish with a little lemon and pepper.

SOUVLAKI

Prep time: 25 minutes

Marinate time: 12 hours

Cook time: 7 minutes

Serves 4

- 2 onions, minced
- 2 cloves garlic, minced
- ¾ cup olive oil, divided
- ½ cup red wine vinegar
- 1 teaspoon dried oregano
- 1¼ pounds lamb shoulder, cut into ¾-inch cubes
- salt and freshly ground pepper, to taste
- 1 packet pita bread, to serve

For the Tzatziki Sauce

- 1¼ cups Greek or Turkish yogurt
- 1 cucumber, cut into 4 sections lengthwise, seeded, and diced to ¼-inch cubes
- 1 small clove garlic, mashed
- 5 sprigs mint, thinned and chopped
- 2 tablespoons olive oil

The day before cooking, toss the onions and garlic in a deep dish with ½ cup of olive oil, vinegar, and oregano. Add the meat cubes and marinate overnight in the refrigerator.

The same day, make the tzatziki. In a salad bowl, combine the yogurt and diced cucumber. Add the garlic, mint, and remaining ⅓ cup of olive oil. Mix everything well.

Grease the griddle with the remaining oil and preheat to high heat. Drain the lamb and sauté for 7 minutes on all sides. Add salt and pepper, to taste.

Serve immediately with the tzatziki and pita bread.

You can find packets of pita in Lebanese, Turkish, or Greek grocery stores, or in supermarkets in the products of the world section.

Braised fennel

Mediterranean Vegetables

Eggplant salad

Grilled spring
vegetables

Grilled summer
vegetables

59

Mediterranean Vegetables

BRAISED FENNEL

Prep time: 5 minutes

Cook time: 20 minutes

Serves 4

- 3 bulbs fennel, halved
- 1 teaspoon baking soda
- 3 tablespoons olive oil
- 3 tablespoons balsamic vinegar
- juice of 2 lemons
- salt and freshly ground pepper, to taste
- ¼ bunch flat-leaf parsley, thinned and chopped

Blanch the fennel bulbs for 15 minutes in a pot of boiling water with the baking soda. Drain.

Grease the griddle with olive oil and preheat to medium heat. Cook the fennel for 2 minutes on each side.

In a bowl, mix the lemon juice with the balsamic vinegar to make a vinaigrette.

Drizzle the braised fennels with the lemon vinaigrette. Add salt and pepper, then sprinkle with the chopped parsley.

EGGPLANT SALAD

Prep time: 10 minutes

Cook time: 10 minutes

Serves 4

- 2 eggplants, cut into ⅔-inch-thick slices.
- 5 tablespoons olive oil
- 1 clove garlic, crushed
- zest and juice of 1 lemon
- salt and freshly ground pepper, to taste
- ¼ bunch basil, thinned and chopped
- ½ cup candied tomatoes

This cooking technique is the simplest way to cook eggplants in oil and allows you to maintain the eggplant's incredible softness.

Brush the eggplants with olive oil.

Marinate the garlic in a bowl with the remaining oil.

On the griddle, cook the eggplants covered at medium heat for 4 to 5 minutes on each side.

While the eggplants are cooking, combine the lemon zest and juice with the garlic-flavored oil, then add in the lemon-garlic marinade to the eggplants.

Let the eggplants cool, then place them on a serving dish. Add salt and pepper, to taste.

Pour the lemon-garlic marinade over the eggplants. Sprinkle with basil and add the candied tomatoes.

This salad pairs well with souvlaki (page 56) or keftas (page 70).

GRILLED SPRING VEGETABLES

Prep time: 10 minutes

Cook time: 12 minutes

Serves 4

- 1 zucchini, cut into 4 sections then sliced into 4 sticks per section
- 4 small new carrots, cut into sticks
- 1 cup snow peas
- ½ cup spring onions
- 1 teaspoon baking soda
- 3 tablespoons olive oil
- salt and freshly ground pepper, to taste

This is the ultimate mid-spring recipe, perfect for celebrating your first outing in the great outdoors after months of confinement. Peas still full of sap and sugar, sweet onions, young carrots—delicious!

Blanch all the vegetables in a pot of boiling water with the baking soda for 5 minutes. Drain them.

Grease the griddle with the olive oil and preheat to medium heat. Color the carrots for 2 minutes on each side. Add the other vegetables and continue cooking for 5 minutes, turning them regularly. Add salt and pepper, to taste.

GRILLED SUMMER VEGETABLES

Prep time: 20 minutes

Cook time: 8 minutes

Serves 4

- 3 tomatoes
- 2 eggplants, thinly sliced lengthwise
- 2 zucchini, thinly sliced lengthwise
- 1 red bell pepper, seeded then cut into ½-inch-wide sticks
- 1 yellow bell pepper, seeded then cut into ½-inch-wide sticks
- 1 green bell pepper, seeded then cut into ½-inch-wide sticks
- 9 tablespoons olive oil, divided
- 1 clove garlic
- ½ bunch basil, chopped
- salt and freshly ground pepper, to taste

Boil the tomatoes for 30 seconds, then put them in cold water; peel and seed them.

Cover the griddle with ¼ cup of olive oil and preheat to medium heat. Cook the vegetables for 3 to 4 minutes per side, adding 2 tablespoons of oil to the griddle when turning them. Add salt and pepper, to taste.

While cooking the vegetables, crush the garlic with the flat side of the knife by pressing and dragging until it becomes a paste. Mix the garlic paste with the remaining oil.

When ready to serve, sprinkle the vegetables with the basil and drizzle with the garlic sauce.

To change up the flavors, add 1 teaspoon of garam masala and replace the basil with cilantro.

FRESH GOAT CHEESE WITH TARRAGON

Prep time: 10 minutes

Cook time: 2 minutes

Serves 4

- 2 tablespoons olive oil
- 4 small logs fresh goat cheese
- zest of 1 lemon
- 2 sprigs tarragon, thinned and chopped
- 4 teaspoons honey

Preheat the griddle to medium heat. Oil a sheet of parchment paper with a brush. Place the goat cheese logs on top and cook on the griddle for 1 minute on each side.

Arrange each log of goat cheese on a separate plate, then sprinkle on the zest and tarragon. Drizzle with honey.

Vary the flavors by replacing the tarragon with mint and the lemon with an orange.

APRICOTS WITH ALMONDS

Prep time: 20 minutes

Cook time: 2 minutes

Serves 4

- 6 Breton shortbread cookies, crushed into a powder
- 2 tablespoons butter, divided
- 6 apricots, pitted and halved
- 2 tablespoons flaked almonds
- 1 cup cherries, pitted and halved
- 10 verbena leaves

Preheat the griddle to medium heat.

Form 1 pile of shortbread powder in the bottom of 4 separate bowls or plates.

Add half of the butter, then the apricots, flesh-side down on the griddle. Cook for 1 minute. Set the apricots aside.

Brown the almonds on the griddle in the remaining butter for 1 minute. Arrange the apricots on the shortbread base. Add the cherries, verbena, and toasted almonds.

To avoid scattering the shortbread crumbs, crush the cookies in a freezer bag or clean dish towel.

CINNAMON APPLES

Prep time: 15 minutes

Cook time: 2 minutes

Serves 4

- 1 tablespoon sugar
- 3 tablespoons butter
- 1 teaspoon ground cinnamon
- 4 golden or yellow apples, peeled and cut into 6 sections each
- 1 teaspoon rum
- 2 tablespoon almonds, crushed
- 2 tablespoons dried cranberries, roughly chopped

Preheat the griddle to medium heat. Caramelize the sugar, then add the butter and cinnamon.

Once the butter has melted, add the apples and rum. Gently stir with a spatula to coat the apples with caramel, then let brown for 1 minute on each side.

Arrange the apples on plates, then sprinkle with the almonds and cranberries.

You can replace the cranberries with raisins or dried apple cubes.

Maghreb and the Middle East

I have a childhood memory of giant pancakes being served for breakfast in Egypt. After the morning meal, the plate was then used to cook meat and fish. This is where I tasted my first Egyptian-style keftas (well garnished with coriander seeds).

SEA BREAM WITH CHERMOULA

Prep time: 20 minutes

Marinate time: 2 hours

Cook time: 30 minutes

Serves 4

- 2 (1¼-pound) sea breams
- 1 cup of chermoula (page 39)

Coat the inside of the sea bream with chermoula (reserve some to make a sauce later). Let marinate for 2 hours.

Preheat the griddle to medium heat. Cook the sea bream for 15 minutes on each side. Serve immediately.

Serve sea bream with braised fennel (see page 60) or couscous with herbs. Use 2 cups of couscous, 2 tablespoons of olive oil, 2 cups of boiling water, 2 tablespoons of chopped fresh cilantro, 1 tablespoon of flat-leaf parsley, 2 sprigs of chopped mint, and the zest of a quarter of a lemon. Pour the olive oil over the couscous, then pour the boiling water over it. Cover for 5 minutes. Fluff the couscous with a fork and mix with the remaining ingredients.

KEFTAS

Prep time: 25 minutes

Cook time: 4 to 6 minutes

Serves 4

- 1¼ pounds lamb shoulder, chopped
- 1 onion, finely chopped
- 1 tablespoon flat-leaf parsley leaves, chopped
- 2 sprigs mint leaves, chopped
- 1 tablespoon coriander seeds
- 2 pinches nutmeg
- 2 pinches ground cinnamon
- 1 pinch cumin
- salt and freshly ground pepper, to taste

These meatballs have as many variations as there are places where they are cooked in the Maghreb and the Middle East. The fatty lamb meat is perfect for this recipe, making it just melt in your mouth.

Preheat the griddle to medium heat.

In a bowl, mix the meat with the chopped onion, parsley, and mint. Add the herbs and spices and knead until a smooth mixture is obtained.

Make 8 keftas by shaping them between the palms of your hands. Pierce them with wooden skewers.

Cook the keftas on the griddle for 4 to 6 minutes, turning them regularly. Add salt and pepper, to taste.

You can replace the lamb with 15% fat beef to prevent the keftas from drying out.

SHAWARMA

Prep time: 25 minutes

Marinade: 24 hours

Cook time: 3 minutes

Serves 4

- 1½ pounds sirloin steak, thinly sliced
- 1 cup shawarma marinade (page 35)
- 3 tablespoons olive oil
- salt and freshly ground pepper, to taste
- 2 tomatoes, sliced
- ½ bunch flat-leaf parsley, stems removed
- 2 malossol pickles, sliced
- ½ cup tarator sauce (page 30)
- 2 bags pita bread, for serving

This dish competes with the real Turkish doner, which features a yogurt and spice marinade (but it is just as good with small pickled peppers). Here, the red wine vinegar and citrus in the marinade enhance the flavor of the beef. Just make sure you drain the meat very well and sear it on a very hot griddle.

Marinate the meat in the shawarma for 24 hours.

Before cooking, drain the meat for 10 minutes and remove the citrus zest, onion, and garlic.

Preheat the griddle to high heat. Cook the meat in the olive oil for 3 minutes, stirring constantly. Add salt and pepper, to taste.

Serve with tomatoes, parsley, pickles, and tarator sauce, with a side of pita bread.

If you don't have malossols, serve with pickles or pickled turnips that you can find in any Asian grocery store.

TAVUK SIS

Prep time: 25 minutes

Marinade: 2 hours

Cook time: 6 minutes

Serves 4

- 3 tablespoons yogurt
- 1 clove garlic, minced
- 2 tablespoons paprika
- 1¼ pounds chicken breasts, cut into strips
- 3 tomatoes, cut into ¼-inch cubes
- 1 cucumber, peeled, seeded, then cut into ¼-inch cubes
- juice of 1 lemon
- 2 tablespoons pomegranate molasses
- ¼ of a red cabbage, chopped
- ½ bunch chopped flat-leaf parsley
- ¼ cup olive oil
- 2 tablespoons butter
- salt and freshly ground pepper, to taste
- 2 tablespoons sumac

This is probably the dish I have eaten the most in Turkey. That little taste of brown butter at the end of each bite...

In a bowl, combine the yogurt, garlic, and paprika. Marinate the chicken strips in the yogurt mixture for 2 hours.

Mix the tomatoes and cucumber with the lemon juice.

Mix the pomegranate molasses with 2 tablespoons of water. Mix the cabbage with three quarters (1½ tablespoons) of the pomegranate molasses and water mixture to make your coleslaw. Combine the rest of the molasses with the parsley.

Grease the griddle with the oil, then cook the chicken strips at medium heat for 3 minutes on each side, adding the butter 1 minute before the end of cooking. Add salt and pepper, to taste.

Serve with coleslaw and cucumber-tomato salad sprinkled with sumac and parsley.

ROASTED FETA WITH TOMATOES

Prep time: 20 minutes

Cook time: 3 minutes

Serves 4

- a few mint leaves, thinned and chopped
- ¼ bunch flat-leaf parsley, thinned and chopped
- zest of 1 lemon
- 2¼ pounds tomatoes
- 2 tablespoons olive oil, plus more to serve
- 14 ounces feta, cut into 4 slices
- ½ cup kalamata olives

Mix the mint, parsley, and lemon zest together and set aside.

Boil the tomatoes for 30 seconds, then immerse them in cold water. Drain, peel, and remove the seeds from the tomatoes. Roughly chop them.

On the griddle, add the olive oil, then cook the feta on one side at medium heat for 1½ minutes. On a different part of the griddle, place the tomatoes. Flip the feta slices over and cook for 1 more minute.

Place the tomatoes on soup plates. Cover with feta, then add the mixture of herbs and lemon zest, olives, and a dash of olive oil.

Enjoy with pita bread or Turkish bread, which you can use to scoop up the tomatoes.

Asia

This chapter will cover three main types of cooking from this geographical area. In Southeast Asia, food is sautéed on a baking sheet or in a wok. The meat is added first, and the vegetables are added at the end of cooking to keep their crunchiness.

For Korean barbecues, strips of meat are simmered with the vegetables and served with an assortment of kimchi and banchans. Finally, the other recipes here include those snacked on in Japan in teppanyaki restaurants, accompanied by vegetables or fried rice.

MEAGRE IN BANANA LEAF

Prep time: 20 minutes

Cook time: 35 minutes

Serves 4

- 6 makrut lime leaves, chopped
- 4 sprigs Thai basil, chopped
- ½ cup lemongrass, first two leaves removed, stems chopped
- 3 inches fresh ginger, peeled and chopped
- ½ cup chopped, fresh coconut
- 1½ inches fresh turmeric, peeled and chopped
- 2 meagre fish, about 1½ pounds
- 13 feet of banana leaves

This is a staple dish from Indonesia. I remember being in a tavern on the island of Lombok. Night was falling, and this little lady gave me this dish with a look that said, "You'll see how good it is." Indeed, this low-calorie dish has an explosion of flavors, and you'll want more as long as there is more. The next day I returned with my notebook and pen, and the lady kindly let me watch her work.

Mix the makrut lime leaves, basil, and lemongrass in a bowl with the ginger, coconut, and turmeric.

Stuff the belly of the fish with this mixture, then firmly wrap each fish in 6½ feet (about half) of the banana leaves. Fold the ends and then the sides and tie them together.

Cook the fish at high heat for 17 minutes on each side. Serve with the remaining stuffing.

If you can't find makrut lime leaves, you can zest the fruit (makrut lime).

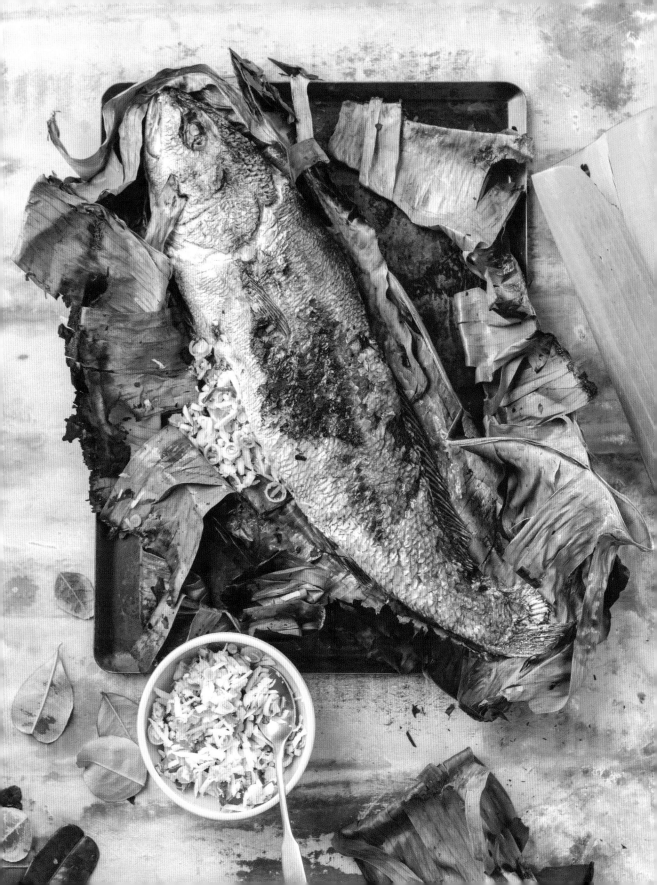

TAMARIND SHRIMP

Prep time: 30 minutes

Cook time: 3 minutes

Serves 4

- 2 tablespoons tamarind paste
- ¼ cup sugar
- 1 bird pepper, sliced
- ½ cup hot water
- 2 tablespoons oil, divided
- 2 pounds raw shrimp, shelled, casings removed
- 1 shallot, minced
- 3 cloves garlic, minced
- ½ cup sliced green onions
- 1 lime
- ½ teaspoon crushed black pepper

This sweet and sour Thai dish was cooked on a canoe and served on the boat I was sitting in. The technique is quite impressive: imagine the cook, on her skiff, with her torso and arm constantly in motion, preparing you a delicious, extra-fresh dish.

In a bowl, mix the tamarind paste, sugar, and pepper with the water.

On the griddle, add 1 tablespoon of olive oil and sauté the shrimp for 1 minute at high heat. Transfer to a plate and set aside.

With the rest of the olive oil, brown the shallot at medium heat, then brown the garlic for 30 seconds.

Place the shrimp back on the griddle, then add the sliced green onions and the tamarind sauce. Continue cooking for 1½ minutes, stirring regularly. Add pepper, to taste, garnish with lime juice, and serve immediately.

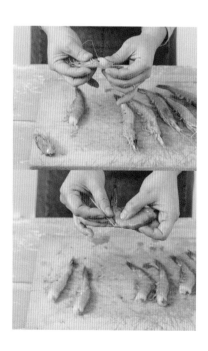

LEMONGRASS PORK RIBS

Prep time: 10 minutes

Marinate time: 2 hours

Cook time: 12 minutes

Serves 4

- 4 pork back ribs, cut into strips
- 3 lemongrass stems, first two leaves removed, stems chopped
- 2 shallots, chopped
- 1 clove garlic, chopped
- 1 tablespoon sugar
- 2 tablespoons fish sauce
- 1 teaspoon five-spice blend
- salt and freshly ground pepper, to taste
- 2 tablespoons ground peanuts
- ¼ bunch cilantro, chopped
- 3 sprigs mint, chopped
- 2 tablespoons sunflower oil

In a bowl, mix the strips of meat with the lemongrass, shallots, garlic, sugar, fish sauce, and spices. Marinate for 2 hours.

Preheat the griddle to high heat. Drain the meat and cook for 6 minutes on each side. Add salt and pepper to taste. Serve with the peanuts and herbs.

If you don't have five-spice blend, mix together 1 teaspoon of Sichuan pepper, 1 teaspoon of cinnamon, 1 teaspoon of star anise, 1 teaspoon of fennel seeds, and ½ teaspoon of cloves.

VIETNAMESE BEER COCKLES

Prep time: 10 minutes

Marinate time: 2 hours

Cook time: 5 minutes

Serves 4

- 1 gallon water
- 1 cup coarse salt
- 5½ pounds cockles
- 1 bird pepper
- juice of 2 limes
- 1 tablespoon sesame oil
- 2 cloves garlic, grated
- 1 teaspoon sugar
- 2 inches fresh ginger, peeled and chopped
- 3¼ cups light beer (Tiger beer, Singha)
- salt and freshly ground pepper, to taste

This is dish is typical of those served in Long Bay in Vietnam. Use whatever the catch of the day is—cockles, in this case. In addition to the magical landscape that inspires it, this dish is famous.

Mix ½ gallon of cold water with ½ cup of coarse salt. Soak the cockles in the salt water for 1 hour to remove any sand inside the shells. Rinse the cockles, then repeat the soaking for 1 more hour with the remaining water and coarse salt. Rinse the cockles with clean water (discard any that are open).

Mix the bird pepper with the lime juice and sesame oil.

Mix the garlic with the sugar.

Cook the cockles on the griddle with the ginger and the garlic-sugar mixture for 5 minutes, basting with beer as you go.

Before serving, pour the pepper, lemon juice, and sesame oil mixture over the cockles. Add salt and pepper, to taste.

SAUTÉED CALAMARI WITH SATAY

Prep time: 30 minutes

Cook time: 4 minutes

Serves 4

- 1¼ pounds calamari
- ½ glass water
- ¼ cup satay
- 1 tablespoon sunflower oil
- 1 cup Napa cabbage, sliced
- 6 stalks celery, tapered and cut on the bias
- salt and freshly ground pepper, to taste
- ¼ cup sliced green onions

Preheat the griddle to high heat.

Wash the calamari, then cut them into large pieces. Make a grid pattern on the flesh using a sharp knife. Dry them.

In a bowl, combine the water and satay.

Add the oil to the griddle, then sauté the calamari for 2 minutes.

Add the cabbage and celery and sauté for 1 minute. Then add the water and satay mixture and stir with a spatula for 30 seconds. Add salt and pepper, to taste.

Transfer everything to the serving dish and sprinkle with green onions.

To prevent the sauce from burning, you can dilute the satay in coconut milk.

GRILLED CARAMEL PORK

Prep time: 20 minutes

Cook time: 25 minutes

Serves 4

- 1½ cups green beans, washed, hulled, and cut into 2 sections
- 2 tablespoons sunflower oil
- 1¼ pounds grilled pork, cut into 1-inch cubes
- ¼ cup brown sugar
- ¼ cup fish sauce
- 1 tablespoon soy sauce
- juice of 1 lime
- 1 red bell pepper, sliced
- 1 tablespoon coriander seeds, crushed
- salt and freshly ground pepper, to taste
- ½ bunch cilantro, chopped

This dish has the sweet and savory effect, with the caramel perfectly balanced by lime and coriander.

Blanch the green beans in a pot of salted boiling water for 15 minutes. Cool the beans under cold water to stop the cooking immediately.

Preheat the griddle to high heat. Add the oil and sauté the meat for 6 minutes. Move it to the side of the griddle. Reheat the beans next to the meat. Lower the heat.

Add the sugar and let it caramelize for a few seconds. Add the fish sauce, soy sauce, and lime juice.

Mix the meat and beans with the caramelized sauce. Add the bell pepper and coriander seeds. Gently mix everything together for 1 minute.

Season with salt and pepper and sprinkle with fresh cilantro.

Serve immediately.

CHICKEN SKEWERS WITH PEANUT SAUCE

Prep time: 20 minutes

Marinate time: 30 minutes

Cook time: 8 minutes

Serves 4

- ¼ cup sweet soy sauce
- ¼ cup apple cider vinegar or rice vinegar
- 1 clove garlic, minced
- 1½ pounds chicken breasts, cut into 1-inch cubes
- 1 cup peanut sauce (page 27)

This is a common street food dish served from Thailand to Malaysia. You even finish the sauce with the rice; it's delicious!

In a bowl, combine the soy sauce, vinegar, and garlic. Pour this mixture into a deep dish.

Add the chicken cubes and let them marinate for 30 minutes.

Drain the chicken cubes and thread them on skewers.

Preheat the griddle to high heat. Place a sheet of parchment paper on top to prevent the sugar from burning. Grill the skewers for 90 seconds per side.

Enjoy the skewers with the peanut sauce.

You can also choose a sweet Thai soy sauce (nam soya, for example) or Indonesian (kecap manis) sauce. The sweet soy sauce offered in Japanese grocery stores is generally less flavorful.

BEEF WITH GREEN PEPPERCORNS

Prep time: 25 minutes

Cook time: 5 minutes

Serves 4

- 1 cup coconut milk
- 2 tablespoons fish sauce
- ½ cup water
- 1 tablespoon red curry paste
- 4 branches green peppercorns
- 2 tablespoons sunflower oil, divided
- 2 bunches bok choy, roughly cut
- 1¼ pounds rump steak, cut into strips
- 1 onion, minced
- ½ bunch Thai basil, chopped

In a bowl, combine the coconut milk, fish sauce, and water. Dilute the curry paste in this mixture, then add the green peppercorns.

Add the oil to the griddle and cook the bok choy for 3 minutes at medium heat. Transfer to a plate and set aside.

Brown the meat and onion with the remaining oil for 1 minute at high heat. Add the bok choy back, then add the coconut milk mixture. Cook for another minute.

Serve immediately with basil sprinkled on top.

If you do not have Thai basil, replace it with European basil and add 1 tablespoon of crushed green anise to the mixture.

JEYUK BOKKEUM
(SPICY KOREAN PORK BBQ)

Prep time: 20 minutes

Marinate time: 1 hour

Cook time: 7 minutes

Serves 4

- 1 inch fresh ginger
- 1 clove garlic
- 1 pound pork loin, sliced thin
- 1 zucchini, sliced
- 2 carrots, peeled and sliced
- 1 onion, sliced
- 2 tablespoons gochujang
- 1 tablespoon sesame oil
- ⅔ cups sake
- 3 tablespoons soy sauce
- 1 teaspoon sugar
- salt and freshly ground pepper, to taste
- ½ cup water
- 5 green onions

This is the easiest Korean dish to cook. The gochujang (be careful, it's very strong!) adds that unique flavor of fermented and spicy grains.

Using a small spoon, mash the ginger with the garlic.

Place the meat and all the sliced vegetables on a platter. Add the garlic-ginger mixture, gochujang, sesame oil, sake, soy sauce, and sugar. Mix and let marinate for 1 hour.

Preheat the griddle to medium heat. Season the marinated meat with salt and pepper. Place it on the griddle, add water and cook for 7 minutes, stirring regularly and making sure the sauce does not spread.

Chop the green onions and sprinkle them on the dish before serving.

Korean grocery stores sell meat already sliced for this dish. If you buy whole meat, put it in the freezer for 1 hour in order to slice it more easily. For this recipe, you can also replace the sake with a dry white wine.

BEEF BULGOGI

Prep time: 20 minutes

Marinate time: 1 hour

Cook time: 4 minutes

Serves 4

- 2 inches fresh ginger
- 3 cloves garlic
- 1 pound rump steak, minced
- 1 onion, minced
- 1 carrot, peeled and minced
- pulp of 1 nashi or comice pear, or ½ glass of pear juice
- 1 tablespoon sesame oil
- 5 tablespoons soy sauce
- salt and freshly ground pepper, to taste
- ¼ cup sesame seeds

Unlike jeyuk bokkeum, this simple dish is very sweet due to nashi pear (however, this type of pear is less flavorful than the comice). This dish is great for everyone who isn't a fan of chile peppers.

Using a small spoon, mash the ginger with the garlic.

Place the minced meat, onion, and carrot on a platter.

Add the garlic-ginger mixture followed by the pear pulp, sesame oil, and soy sauce. Mix and let marinate for 1 hour.

Preheat the griddle to medium heat. Salt and pepper, to taste. Place the marinated meat on the griddle and cook for 4 minutes, stirring regularly. Sprinkle with sesame seeds before serving.

SHELLFISH TEPPANYAKI

Prep time: 30 minutes

Cook time: 7 minutes

Serves 4

- 12 large raw shrimp (like tiger prawns)
- ¼ cup mirin
- ¼ cup sake
- 4 scallops
- 3 tablespoons sunflower oil, divided
- ½ cup water
- 1 clove garlic, minced
- salt and freshly ground pepper, to taste

Try to get the seafood ingredients as fresh as possible; that will help the dish taste more authentic. This is a very simple dish with few additions, and the quality of the product is paramount.

Remove the last ring from the tails of the shrimp, then remove the casings with a toothpick. Preserve the shells.

Mix the mirin and the sake.

On the griddle set to high heat, cook the scallops in half the oil for 2 minutes on each side. Then set them to one side of the griddle.

Lower the griddle to medium heat, place the shrimp in two tight rows, then press them down with a baking sheet to prevent the shrimp from contracting. Pour in the water and cover. Cook for 1 minute.

Brown the garlic with the rest of the oil.

Marinate the scallops in the sake-mirin mixture for 30 seconds, then place them on a dish. Season with pepper, to taste, and keep warm.

Using a spatula, continue cooking the shrimp for 1 minute with the shells in the oil-garlic mixture. Add salt and pepper, to taste. Place the shrimp tails on the dish with the scallops and serve.

YAKITORI

Prep time: 20 minutes
Marinate time: 1 hour
Cook time: 8 minutes

Serves 4

- 6 boneless, skinless chicken thighs
- 2 green onions
- ¾ inch fresh ginger, chopped
- 1 teaspoon sesame oil
- 3 thin leeks, cut into 1-inch sticks
- ¾ cup shiitake mushrooms, halved

For the marinade

- 1 clove garlic, chopped
- ½ inch fresh ginger, chopped
- 10 tablespoons soy sauce
- ¼ cup sugar
- 2 tablespoons cider vinegar or rice vinegar

Make the marinade: mix the garlic and ginger in a bowl with the rest of the marinade ingredients.

Cut the chicken into strips and skewer them. Soak all the chicken skewers in half the marinade for 1 hour.

Skewer the leeks widthwise.

Skewer the shiitake mushrooms onto two wooden skewers so that they can easily be turned.

Soak the leek and shiitake skewers for 1 hour in the rest of the marinade.

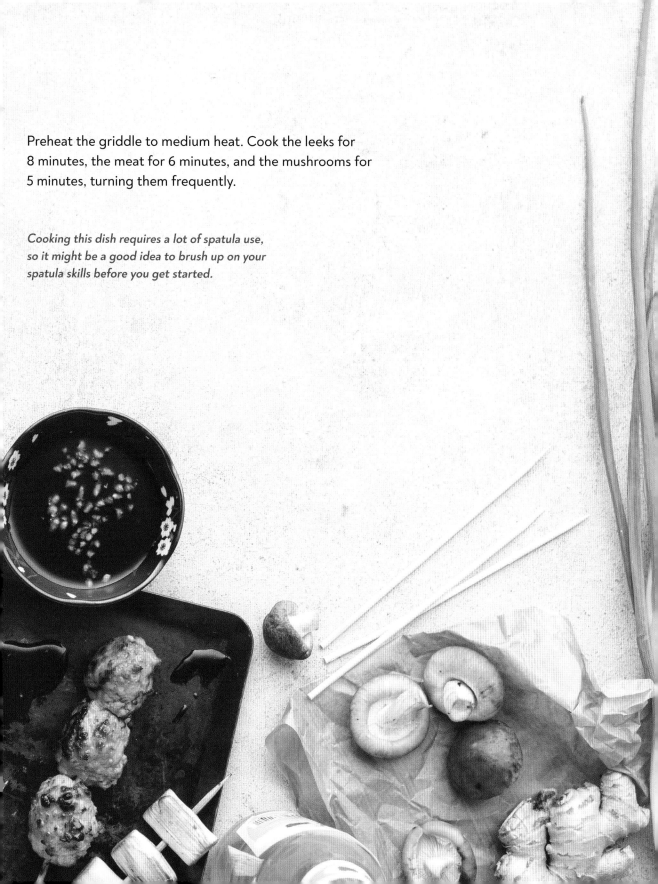

Preheat the griddle to medium heat. Cook the leeks for
8 minutes, the meat for 6 minutes, and the mushrooms for
5 minutes, turning them frequently.

*Cooking this dish requires a lot of spatula use,
so it might be a good idea to brush up on your
spatula skills before you get started.*

PONZU CLAMS

Prep time: 15 minutes

Cook time: 5 minutes

Serves 4

- 4½ pounds clams
- ¼ cup yuzu juice or juice of 1 lime
- ½ cup soy sauce
- ¼ cup mirin
- ¼ cup sake
- 6 onions, chopped

This is one of my favorite dishes. Simple, light, with the unique flavor of yuzu to really enhance the flavor of the shellfish.

Preheat the griddle to medium heat.

Rinse the clams thoroughly to remove any sand residue (discard the open ones).

In a bowl, mix the yuzu juice with the soy sauce, mirin, and sake to make the ponzu sauce.

Place the clams on the griddle and cook them with the ponzu sauce for 5 minutes, covered. Sprinkle with onions just before serving.

You can spice up this dish even more by making a dashi broth to add to the other ingredients: in a saucepan, boil 1 cup of water with 1 piece of kombu and a handful of dried bonito, then filter.

TAMARIND HANGER STEAK

Prep time: 15 minutes

Cook time: 7 minutes

Serves 4

- ¾ inch fresh ginger, cut into sticks
- 1 red onion, chopped
- 2 sprigs mint, chopped
- ½ bunch cilantro, chopped
- 1 stalk celery, finely chopped
- 1 tablespoon soy sauce
- 2 tablespoons tamarind puree
- 1¼ pounds hanger steak
- salt and freshly ground pepper, to taste

I tasted this dish after crossing the border into Vietnam. It was a real pleasure after an hours-long bus ride in the company of soldiers, who were little inclined to laugh. I filmed the chef cooking this dish so I wouldn't forget the recipe!

Preheat the griddle to high heat.

In a bowl, mix the ginger, onion, mint, cilantro, and celery with the soy sauce and tamarind puree.

Sear the meat for 1 minute on each side. Then lower the heat to medium and continue cooking for 2 to 3 minutes on each side. Add salt and pepper, to taste. Serve immediately with the sauce.

You can also serve this dish with sautéed rice: make the rice with 2 handfuls of bean sprouts, 4 chopped green onions, 1 clove of garlic, and 1 tablespoon of soy sauce.

LAMB CHOPS WITH CHILE PEPPERS

Prep time: 15 minutes

Marinate time: 12 hours

Cook time: 6 minutes

Serves 4

- 1 inch fresh ginger
- 1 clove garlic
- 2 chile peppers, chopped
- 1 cup Greek or Turkish yogurt
- juice of 2 limes
- 1 teaspoon garam masala
- 8 lamb chops
- salt and freshly ground pepper, to taste

Mash the ginger with the garlic. Mix the ginger, garlic, and peppers together in a bowl with the yogurt, lime juice, and garam masala.

In a deep dish, marinate the lamb chops in this mixture overnight.

Preheat the griddle to high heat. Place a sheet of greased parchment paper on top of the griddle and sear the meat for 3 minutes per side. Add salt and pepper, to taste.

To spice up and add color to this dish, add 1 tablespoon of paprika and 1 teaspoon of organic turmeric powder (or ½-inch of grated fresh turmeric).

CHICKEN TIKKA

Prep time: 20 minutes

Marinate time: 3 hours

Cook time: 6 minutes

Serves 4

- 1½ pounds chicken breasts, cut into 1-inch cubes
- 1 cup tikka marinade (page 34)
- 1½ cups Greek or Turkish yogurt
- 1 teaspoon garam masala
- 1 teaspoon ground turmeric
- salt and freshly ground pepper, to taste
- ¼ bunch cilantro

Place the chicken in a deep dish and cover it with the tikka marinade. Marinate for 3 hours. Then add the yogurt, garam masala, and turmeric.

Spear the chicken cubes onto skewers and let the excess marinade drain off.

Preheat the griddle to medium heat. Place a sheet of greased parchment paper on the griddle, then add the skewers on top. Cook the skewers for 3 minutes on each side. Add salt and pepper, to taste. Sprinkle with chopped cilantro when ready to serve.

You can make your own homemade garam masala with 1 teaspoon of coriander seeds, 1 teaspoon of cumin seeds, 1 teaspoon of black peppercorns, ½ teaspoon of nutmeg, 1 clove, and ½ bay leaf. Roast all of the ingredients for 30 seconds at medium heat then reduce them to a powder.

CHOP SUEY VEGETABLES

Prep time: 15 minutes

Cook time: 5 minutes

Serves 4

- 3 tablespoons sunflower oil
- 1½ inches fresh ginger, grated
- 5 tablespoons soy sauce
- 2 tablespoons oyster sauce
- ½ cup water
- 1 tablespoon sugar
- ⅓ Napa cabbage (preferably the base of the vegetable), sliced
- 1 yellow onion, minced
- 2 carrots, cut into ¼-inch slices
- 1 clove garlic, minced
- ½ cup bean sprouts
- 4 green onions, chopped

A classic of Chinese-American cuisine, this simple dish gives you the perfect pairing of flavors: fresh vegetables alongside a delicious grilling.

Preheat the griddle to high heat with the sunflower oil.

In a bowl, mix the ginger with the soy sauce, oyster sauce, water, and sugar.

Sauté the cabbage, onion, and carrots on the griddle for 2 minutes.

Add the garlic and bean sprouts and cook for 1 minute, stirring regularly. Pour the sauce over the vegetables, coating them well. Cook for 1 more minute, stirring constantly.

Garnish with the green onions and serve immediately.

SPICED CAULIFLOWER

Prep time: 15 minutes

Cook time: 8 to 13 minutes

Serves 4

- 3 tomatoes
- 1 tablespoon tamarind puree
- ⅔ cup water
- 1 onion, chopped
- 3 tablespoons oil, divided
- 1 inch fresh turmeric, chopped into thin sticks, or 1 teaspoon organic turmeric powder
- 1 tablespoon yellow mustard seeds, crushed
- 1 tablespoon black mustard seeds, crushed
- 1 tablespoon coriander seeds, crushed
- 1 teaspoon ground cumin
- 1 head cauliflower, broken into florets
- salt and freshly ground pepper, to taste

This dish will make you absolutely love cauliflower. Choose a small cauliflower and make sure to follow the cooking times. Overcooking cauliflower can bring out an unpleasant sulfurous taste.

Boil the tomatoes for 30 seconds. Drain them, then remove the skin and seeds; cut them into ¼-inch cubes.

Preheat the griddle to medium heat.

In a bowl, combine the tamarind puree and water.

Brown the onion in 1 tablespoon of oil for 1 minute. Then move the onion to one side of the griddle.

With the remaining oil, roast all the spices for 30 seconds, then mix them with the onions. Immediately add the cauliflower and let it brown for 1 minute.

Add the tomatoes and the diluted tamarind puree. Add salt and pepper, to taste.

Cover the vegetables and cook for 5 to 10 more minutes, making sure that the vegetables do not stick.

You can substitute the cauliflower with green beans—just precook the beans for 10 minutes in boiling water.

Teppanyaki
vegetables

Nasi goreng
(Indonesian fried rice)

Fried Rice

Shrimp fried rice

Fried Rice

TEPPANYAKI VEGETABLES

Prep time: 10 minutes
Cook time: 30 minutes

Serves 4

- 1 cup rice
- 3 tablespoons sunflower oil
- 2 inches fresh ginger, grated
- 3 tablespoons soy sauce
- ¼ cup sake
- 1 tablespoon sesame oil
- ½ Napa cabbage, sliced
- 2 carrots, peeled and cut into ¼-inch-thick slices
- 1 cup bean sprouts
- 6 green onions, sliced
- 1 clove garlic, mashed

Cook the rice according to the directions on the package. Drain.

Preheat the griddle to medium heat with the sunflower oil.

In a bowl, mix the ginger with the soy sauce, sake, and sesame oil.

Using a spatula, sauté the vegetables on the griddle for 3 minutes. Add the garlic and rice and continue cooking for 2 minutes. Pour the sauce over the vegetables and cook for 1 minute while stirring.

SHRIMP FRIED RICE

Prep time: 10 minutes
Cook time: 30 minutes

Serves 4

- 2¼ cups jasmine rice
- 2 eggs
- 3 tablespoons sunflower oil, divided
- 1 tablespoon soy sauce
- 1 tablespoon oyster sauce
- 2 tablespoons fish sauce
- freshly ground pepper
- 2 yellow onions, chopped
- 1¼ pounds raw shrimp, shelled and casings removed with a toothpick
- 2 cloves garlic, mashed
- 5 green onions, sliced

Cook the rice according to the instructions on the package.

Preheat the griddle to medium heat.

Beat the eggs like you would to make an omelet.

Using 1 tablespoon of oil, cook the eggs like an omelet for 1 minute, spreading them very thinly. Roll up the eggs using a spatula, and slice. Reserve on a plate.

In a bowl, combine the soy sauce, oyster sauce, and fish sauce. Season with the freshly ground pepper.

On the griddle, brown the onions with the remaining oil for 2 minutes at medium heat. Add the shrimp and cook for 2 more minutes. Finally, add the garlic, green onions, the well-drained rice, and the sauce. Continue cooking for 1 minute.

NASI GORENG (INDONESIAN FRIED RICE)

Prep time: 20 minutes

Cook time: 15 to 20 minutes

Serves 4

- 2¼ cups jasmine rice
- 3 eggs
- 5 tablespoons sunflower oil, divided
- 1 teaspoon shrimp paste
- ¼ cup water
- ⅔ pound pork loin, cut into strips
- 2 yellow onions, chopped
- 2 cloves garlic, mashed
- ⅔ pound raw shrimp, shelled, casings removed with a toothpick
- 6 green onions
- 2 tablespoons soy sauce
- freshly ground pepper, to taste

This stir-fried rice can be found all over Indonesia, along with its noodle variant, mi goreng. It can be made with or without pork, depending on the island you are on. It's the perfect dish to eat in the street, in between trips in a mini-van and accompanied by a lemonade or a light beer.

Cook the rice according to the directions on the package. Drain and set aside near the griddle.

Preheat the griddle to medium heat.

Beat the eggs like you would for an omelet.

In 1 tablespoon of oil, cook the beaten eggs for 1 minute, spreading them very thinly. Roll the eggs up with the spatula and cut into thin strips. Reserve on a plate.

Dilute the shrimp paste with the water.

Cook the pork and onions in 2 tablespoons of oil for 4 minutes at high heat, stirring often. Add the garlic, shrimp, and diluted shrimp paste. Continue cooking for 1 minute while stirring.

Add the remaining oil, eggs, rice, green onions, and soy sauce. Cook for another 2 minutes. Finally, add pepper, to taste.

When cooking rice, the most practical way is to use a rice cooker (pressure cooker rice). You can also cook the rice in a saucepan.

To prevent the rice from drying out while cooking on the griddle, add a little bit of water when cooking.

GRILLED PINEAPPLE

Prep time: 10 minutes

Cook time: 3 minutes

Serves 4

- 2 tablespoons butter
- ½ inch fresh ginger, sliced into thin sticks
- 1 pineapple, peeled, cored, and cut into ½-inch-thick slices
- lime ice cream, to serve
- ¾ inch fresh turmeric, cut into thin sticks
- 2 sprigs mint, stripped
- 6 passion fruits, halved, insides removed

Preheat the griddle to medium heat.

Melt the butter with the ginger, then sear the pineapple slices for 90 seconds on each side.

Arrange the roasted pineapple slices on plates. Top with a scoop of lime ice cream. Sprinkle with turmeric and mint leaves, and add the passion fruit around the edges.

America and the Caribbean

Contrary to legend, South America isn't filled with just barbecue lovers! The most emblematic example is the Mexican comal that is exported to Honduras and Nicaragua—a large round plate on which the natives cook tortillas and the meat that goes with them.

The griddle is also found in Peru and Colombia. Grilled meats in these parts are served with aji (a spicy garlic sauce with a thousand variations). Even Argentinians cook certain dishes on griddles placed on their barbecues.

BARBECUE SIRLOIN STEAK

Prep time: 2 minutes

Cook time: 5 to 10 minutes

Serves 4

- ¼ cup olive oil
- 4 sirloin fillets
- salt and freshly ground pepper, to taste
- 1 cup barbecue sauce (page 27)

Grease the griddle with the oil and preheat it to high heat.

Sear the meat at high heat for 2 minutes on each side.

Lower the griddle to medium heat and cook for 30 more seconds per side for rare meat; 1½ more minutes per side for medium meat; 3 more minutes per side for well-done meat.

Add salt and pepper, to taste. Serve the meat hot with the barbecue sauce.

ONION STEAK

Prep time: 2 minutes

Cook time: 8 to 12 minutes

Serves 4

- ¼ cup olive oil
- 4 rump steaks, about 6 ounces each
- salt and freshly ground pepper, to taste
- 1 cup onion sauce (page 31)

Grease the griddle with the oil and preheat it to high heat.

Sear the meat at high heat for 2 minutes on each side.

Lower the griddle to medium heat and cook for 2 more minutes per side for rare meat; 3 more minutes per side for medium meat; 4 more minutes per side for well-done meat.

Add salt and pepper, to taste. Serve the meat hot with the onion sauce.

CHURRASCO RIB EYE

Prep time: 40 minutes

Marinate time: 6 hours

Cook time: 6 to 12 minutes

Serves 4

- 2 (1-pound) rib eye steaks
- 1 cup churrasco marinade (page 35)
- 2 tablespoons olive oil
- salt and freshly ground pepper, to taste

Marinate the meat in the churrasco marinade for 6 hours.

Grease the griddle with the oil and preheat it to high heat.

Drain the meat, then sear it at high heat for 2 minutes on each side.

Lower the griddle to medium heat and cook for 1 more minute per side for rare meat; 2½ more minutes per side for medium meat; 4 more minutes per side for well-done meat.

Add salt and pepper, to taste. Serve the meat hot with chimichurri sauce (page 30).

CHICKEN CHURRASCARIA

Prep time: 20 minutes

Marinate time: 2 hours

Cook time: 11 minutes

Serves 4

- 6 chicken thighs, deboned
- 2 cups churrascaria marinade (page 38)
- salt and freshly ground pepper, to taste

Marinate the chicken thighs in the churrascaria marinade for 2 hours.

Preheat the griddle to medium heat.

Drain the chicken thighs and cook them, skin-side down, for 7 minutes. Finish cooking for 4 minutes on the flesh side.

Add salt and pepper, to taste.

You can accompany the chicken with adobo sauce (page 31) or dog sauce (page 26).

CHICKEN TORTILLAS

Prep time: 45 minutes

Marinate time: 3 hours

Cook time: 10 minutes

Serves 4

For garnish

- 2 cloves garlic, minced
- 1 onion, minced
- 1 chile pepper, sliced
- 5 boneless, skinless chicken thighs, cut into very small cubes
- juice of 2 limes
- 1 teaspoon ground cumin
- 1 teaspoon dried oregano
- 1 bay leaf
- 2 tablespoons olive oil, for cooking

For the tortillas

- 1½ cups all-purpose flour
- 1 packet yeast
- 1 teaspoon salt
- 1 teaspoon sugar
- ¼ cup lard or 2½ tablespoons olive oil
- ⅔ cup hot water

For the salsa

- 4 tomatoes, seeded and diced
- 1 red onion, diced
- ¼ bunch cilantro, chopped
- juice of 1 lime
- salt, to taste

Prepare the garnish. Mix the garlic, onion, and chile in a bowl with the chicken. Add the lime juice, cumin, oregano, and bay leaf. Let marinate for 3 hours in the refrigerator.

Make the tortillas. In a bowl, combine the flour, yeast, salt, sugar, oil, and hot water. Work the dough for 5 minutes until it is smooth. Cover and let stand for 1 hour in a warm place.

Prepare the salsa. Mix the tomatoes, onion, and cilantro in a large bowl, then add the lime juice and salt. Set aside.

Divide the dough into 4 balls. Divide each ball in half to make 8 balls. Roll each of these out with a little flour to form 6-inch discs.

Preheat the griddle to medium heat. Cook the tortillas with a little lard or olive oil for 1 minute on the first side and 30 seconds on the second, then set aside. Cook the chicken at high heat in olive oil for 4 minutes, stirring constantly.

To serve, garnish the tortillas with the chicken and salsa.

You can add sliced avocado or grated cheddar cheese to the freshly cooked meat.

SEA BREAM FILLET WITH MANGO SAUCE

Prep time: **15 minutes**

Cook time: **7 minutes**

Serves 4

- 4 fillets of pink, royal, or gray sea bream
- 1 cup mango sauce (page 26)
- 2 tablespoons olive oil

Preheat the griddle to medium heat.

Oil the griddle, then cook the fillets skin-side down for 7 minutes.

Serve the fillets topped with mango sauce.

Avoid farmed gilthead sea bream, which is less tasty and less firm than wild sea bream. Otherwise, use pink sea bream, which has a taste very similar to that of the royal or gray sea bream. The gray sea bream is often very inexpensive.

SEA BASS WITH DOG SAUCE

Prep time: 20 minutes

Cook time: 30 minutes

Serves 4

- 2 tablespoons olive oil
- 2 sea bass (1½ pounds)
- 1 cup dog sauce (page 26)

Preheat the griddle to medium heat.

Place a sheet of parchment paper on the griddle and oil it. Place the sea bass on top and cook for 15 minutes per side.

Serve the sea bass with the dog sauce.

You can also serve this dish with mashed sweet potatoes. To make them, use 1 pound of sweet potatoes, 1 pound of potatoes, ¼ cup of butter, and 1½ cups of milk.

Peel the vegetables and cut them into ¼-inch cubes. Cook them for 20 minutes in boiling water, and then mash them. Add the milk, then the butter at the end of cooking. Add salt and pepper, to taste. You can also add ¼ cup of candied lemon to spice up this dish.

PORK LOIN CHOPS WITH CUBAN MOJO SAUCE

Prep time: 15 minutes

Cook time: 16 minutes

Serves 4

- 1 tablespoon olive oil
- 4 pork loin chops
- salt and freshly ground pepper, to taste
- 1 cup mojo sauce (page 27)

A friend from Cuba introduced me to this sauce. I didn't think it could be so tasty, miles from the Caribbean Sea and without the scorching island sun. It was the full package!

Preheat the griddle to high heat.

Oil the griddle, then sear the meat for 1 minute on each side. Then lower to medium heat and continue cooking for 7 more minutes per side.

Season the meat with salt and pepper to taste. Serve it hot with the mojo sauce.

Add more depth to this dish by serving it with fresh corn that is sliced from the cob, cooked on the griddle, and seasoned with a little salted butter.

RIB EYE WITH ADOBO SAUCE

Prep time: 2 minutes

Cook time: 6 to 12 minutes

Serves 4

- 2 tablespoons olive oil
- 2 (1-pound) rib eye steaks
- salt and freshly ground pepper, to taste
- 1 cup adobo sauce (page 31)

Grease the griddle with the oil and preheat to high heat.

Sear the meat at high heat for 2 minutes on each side.

Lower the griddle to medium heat and cook for 1 additional minute per side for rare meat; 2½ additional minutes per side for medium meat; 4 additional minutes per side for well-done meat.

Season the meat with salt and pepper, to taste. Serve it hot with the adobo sauce.

Adobo sauce also goes very well with a well-grilled, crispy pork loin. If the pepper makes the sauce too spicy, add a little sugar to balance it out.

BANANAS WITH RUM

Prep time: 10 minutes

Cook time: 8 minutes

Serves 4

- zest and juice of 1 lime
- 4 bananas
- 2 tablespoons butter
- 3 tablespoons rum
- 1 firm, ripe mango, cut into strips

This is a traditional end-of-meal dish. It requires little preparation and is even better with fressinette bananas.

Preheat the griddle to medium heat.

Mix the lime zest and juice together.

Brown the bananas in their skin for 3 minutes on each side. Cut them in half lengthwise then, with the butter, cook them again for 2 minutes on the flesh side.

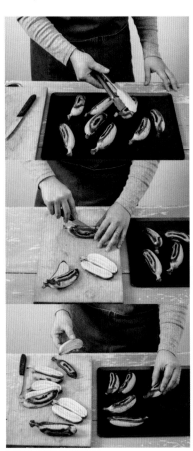

Deglaze the bananas with the rum. Flip the bananas and, using a spatula, distribute the rum over the flesh.

Arrange the half-bananas on plates, with the flesh side up. Sprinkle with the lime juice and zest, then add the mango slices.

You can add crushed peanuts to give this dish a more gourmet quality, or grated turmeric to lighten the taste of the banana.

Resources

National grocery store chains often have an aisle with Asian products. Also, check for local stores specializing in items from a particular country or region.

GENERAL FOOD STORES
Whole Foods
Locations across the US and online
www.wholefoodsmarket.com

SPECIALTY FOOD STORES
Patel Brothers (Indian)
Locations across the US
www.patelbros.com

H Mart (Korean)
Locations across the US
www.hmart.com

Mitsuwa Marketplace (Japanese)
Locations: California, Illinois, New Jersey, Texas, and Hawaii
www.mitsuwa.com

99 Ranch Market (Chinese, Taiwanese, Southeast Asian)
Locations: California, Maryland, Massachusetts, Nevada, New Jersey, Oregon, Texas, Virginia, Washington, and online
www.99ranch.com

Tulumba (Turkish)
Online store only: www.tulumba.com

Greek International Market (Greek and Mediterranean)
Locations: Boston, Massachusetts, and online
www.madfeta.com

Kalamala (Middle Eastern)
Online store only: kalamala.com

Cardenas Market (Latin American)
Locations: California, Las Vegas, and Arizona
www.cardenasmarkets.com

Acknowledgments

Thanks to Marie, Niels, and Jan for their curiosity. To Anne la Fay and Aurélie Cazenave for their confidence. To Blandine Hanauer for her good humor and patience.

Chae Rin Vincent would like to thank the following brands and shops who were kind enough to provide him with the articles necessary for the production of this book: Eno Groupe, www.eno.fr ; Les Guimards, www.lesguimards.com; and Petit Pan, www.petitpan.com.